A Very Brief Introduction to Futures

João Teixeira

Contents

About the author   v

1 Introduction   1

2 Futures? What is that?   3

3 Futures versus forwards   7
    3.1 The unique case of the London Metals Exchange . . .   9

4 Futures contracts specifications   11

5 Market participants   17

6 Margins and daily settlement   23
    6.1   Leverage and Risks in Futures Trading 27

7 Settlement and delivery   31

8 Futures exchanges and clearinghouses   41
    8.1   Futures exchanges 41

    8.2   Clearinghouses 44

9 Final remarks   47

About the author

João Teixeira holds an MSc in Operational Research from Universidade de Lisboa and a degree in economics from Universidade Técnica de Lisboa.

João has worked in the Managed Futures industry since 2002 and has held the following roles:

- Consultant since 2022 at Tolomeo Capital AG, a Zurich based systematic asset manager.

- Partner, Chief Risk Officer and Research Director, from 2013 to 2022, at Solaise Capital Management a London based systematic asset manager.

- Senior researcher, from 2008 to 2011, at Aspect Capital, a London based systematic asset manager.

- Senior quantitative researcher, from 2002 to 2007, at Winton Capital Management a London based systematic asset manager.

Chapter 1

Introduction

The purpose of this book is to provide a concise introduction to futures markets.

One of the main challenges in writing a book like this is determining the best way to organize chapters, given the interlinked nature of topics. Hopefully this text will have at least an acceptable flow. Still some issues are inevitable. For instance, we discuss futures exchanges before Section 8.1, which formally defines and lists the most significant futures exchanges.

I will use bullet points generously, as I find they work very well at presenting memorable, clear and succinct information.

In Chapter 2, I cover the fundamentals of futures contracts, including examples of common products. Chapter 3 examines the differences between futures and forwards, while Chapter 4 focuses on futures contract specifications. In Chapter 5, we discuss the primary participants in the futures markets. Chapter 6 explains margins and mark to market procedures, with further details on daily settlement and delivery in Chapter 7. Chapter 8 introduces the major futures exchanges and clearinghouses. Finally, Chapter 9 offers closing remarks.

Some quantative examples are presented in the text, note that none of them takes into consideration transaction costs which are beyond the scope of this text.

This text has been formatted for two sided printing.

Chapter 2

Futures? What is that?

What is a futures contract? A futures contract is a legally binding agreement between two parties. One party agrees to buy, and the other agrees to sell a commodity or financial instrument at a fixed price on a specified future date. Futures contracts are typically traded in an exchange (see section 8.1 for a list of exchanges) and standardized (see chapter 4).

Futures contracts generally fall into two main categories: Commodities and Financials.

Commodities can be defined as basic, raw materials or primary agricultural products that can be bought, sold, or traded. Commodities are generally interchangeable with other goods of the same type, meaning they are fungible (one unit of a commodity is essentially the same as another). Commodities can, for instance, be:

- Agricultural products like:
  - Cocoa [20].
  - Rapeseed [18].
- Energy products like:
  - Gasoil [23].
  - Natural gas [6].
- Industrial and precious metal products like:
  - Gold [10].
  - Platinum [13].

Trading industrial metals like aluminium, tin, zinc, etc., can be a bit more complicated since the London Metals Exchange (LME) - see section 3.1 which is the main base metals exchange does not trade futures as such, but an hybrid between futures and forward contracts (these instruments will be discussed in chapter 3).

Nevertheless, some other exchanges trade base metals futures and one example is the Multi Commodity Exchange (MCX) [28] in India (see chapter 8.1 for a list of exchanges).

Financial products are futures contracts based on non-physical assets or metrics, providing exposure to financial markets. These products are traded as futures contracts and enable investors to gain exposure to changes in various financial markets, such as:

- Equity products like:

- E-mini Nasdaq-100 [7].
- Hang Seng Index [19].

- Currency products like:
    - Mexican peso Futures [11].
    - Euro FX futures [9].

- Fixed income products (bonds and short term interest rates) like:
    - SGX 10 Year Full-sized Japanese Government Bond Futures [29].
    - Long Gilt Futures [22].

When an investor buys futures contracts it is said that went long. Conversely if an investor sells futures contracts is said that went short.

It is common to instead of saying buying/selling 1 futures contract saying buying/selling 1 lot. So one could say: I went long 2 lots of Rubber [26] or I went short 4 lots of KOSPI 200 Futures [27] Note that the number of contracts bought or sold is always an integer number. It is not possible to buy or sell a fractional number of contracts.

Futures markets have appeared in Hollywood movies. My favourite is the 1983 movie Trading places starring Dan Aykroyd, Jamie Lee Curtis and Eddie Murphy. The main product featured in this movie is frozen concentrated orange juice [21] which is traded on Intercontinental Exchange (ICE) (see chapter 8.1 for a list of exchanges).

Chapter 3

Futures versus forwards

Both forward and futures contracts are agreements to buy or sell an asset in the future at a predetermined price. Key differences between them include:

- A forward contract is settled at the end of the contract term, while a futures contract has standardized expiration dates and is marked to market daily (see chapter 6). For example:
    - Take the rough rice [14] contract ending in November 2024 listed on the Chicago Mercantile exchange (CME) (see chapter 8.1 for a list of exchanges). This contract has a fixed expiry: The business day prior to 15th of November, which is Thursday the 14th of November. So at the time of writing this paragraph (14th of October, 2024) there are 30 days until the contract expires. On October 15, there will be only 29 days until this contract expires.

- In the case of a forward, if we buy a 30 day forward it will expire in 30 days. Tomorrow this contract will not be available to trade any more. Tomorrow a new 30 day forward will be available.

- Futures contracts involve daily settlement, or marking to market, where gains and losses are realized incrementally until expiration (see chapter 6). In contrast, forwards typically settle only once, at the end of the contract term, without daily adjustments. This distinction between end of contract settlement and daily settlement is crucial.

- Futures are standardised contracts (see chapter 4), mainly exchange traded (see section 8.1 for a list of exchanges), where the quality, quantity and both delivery time and location are defined.

- Forward contracts tend to be products traded over the counter that can be tailored to exactly meet the buyer and seller needs.

In summary, both futures and forwards are binding agreements to buy or sell an asset at a set price in the future, but there are a few essential differences between them. Futures are standardised contracts traded on exchange (see chapter 4) and, consequently, non negotiable. Forwards contracts are mainly non standardised contracts traded over the counter, whose terms need to negotiated between buyer and seller.

3.1 The unique case of the London Metals Exchange

The London Metals Exchange (LME) takes a unique approach to futures contracts, combining features of both typical futures and forwards.

In most futures markets, contracts are standardized with fixed monthly expiration dates, and are marked to market daily. But on the LME, futures contracts have more flexibility in terms of expiration and settlement, combining features of both futures and forwards:

- Flexible Expiration Dates: LME futures have daily expiration dates out to 3 months, then weekly expiries out to 6 months, and monthly dates out to 10 years.

- Daily Settlement (Mark to Market - see chapter 6): Like other futures markets, LME contracts are also marked to market daily. However, the actual settlement (physical or cash settlement - see chapter 7) is only done at the contract's expiration date.

- Prompt Dates: The LME uses what are called prompt dates, which are custom expiration dates aligned to the buyer's or seller's needs. This flexibility gives the LME a hybrid characteristic between typical futures and forward contracts.

- So, while LME futures do follow the standard futures practice of daily marking to market, they also offer unique flexibility in contract duration and settlement dates.

One example in relation to expiration dates. On the 14th of October 2024 it is possible, for instance, to buy a 3 month contract ending on the 14th of January 2025. On the 15th of October this contract is not available any more. Instead we can buy another contract ending on the 15th of January 2025. This means that unlike normal futures LME futures are settled only once at the end of the contract term.

This unique settlement structure impacts risk management. While investors in typical futures can easily adjust exposure by closing positions before expiration, LME contracts can only be settled upon expiration, limiting short-term risk mitigation.

Chapter 4

Futures contracts specifications

Futures contracts follow rigorous specifications which exchanges define to standardize trading. Key specifications include:

- contract size,
- currency used,
- exact definition of product quality (especially important for commodities, but also for fixed income),
- trading hours,
- minimum price fluctuation (also called tick size),
- contract months,

- settlement method,

- first notice day, and

- last trading day.

The standardization of futures contracts simplifies trading by removing the need to negotiate terms such as quantity, quality, delivery time, or location.

Table 4.1 shows the specifications for the Swiss franc futures [15] listed on the CME (see section 8.1 for a list of exchanges).

We can see in table 4.1 that the contract size is 125,000 Swiss francs (CHF). Consequently if we buy 1 Swiss franc futures contract we are buying 125,000 Swiss francs. At the time and date of writing this paragraph the price for the December 2024 contract was 1.1778 USD (meaning 1.1778 USD buys 1 Swiss franc). So the price of one contract was $1.1778 \times 125,000 = 147,225$ USD.

This contract is traded both on CME Globex and CME ClearPort. These are two distinct electronic platforms provided by the CME group (see section 8.1 for a list of exchanges) each serving a different function in the trading and clearing process:

- CME Globex is the trading platform, where users actively buy and sell contracts, whereas CME ClearPort is a clearing and post-trade processing platform designed for off-exchange or customized trades.

- CME Globex is best for standard contracts and almost 24/7

Contract Unit	125,000 Swiss francs
Price Quotation	U.S. dollars and cents per CHF increment
Trading Hours	CME Globex: Sunday - Friday 6:00 p.m. - 5:00 p.m. (5:00 p.m. - 4:00 p.m. CT) with a 60-minute break each day beginning at 5:00 p.m. (4:00 p.m. CT) CME ClearPort: 5:00 p.m. - Friday 5:45 p.m. CT with no reporting Monday Sunday - Thursday from 5:45 p.m. - 6:00 p.m. CT
Minimum Price Fluctuation	CME Globex: 0.00005 CHF increment = $6.25 Calendar spreads: 0.00005 CHF increment = $6.25 CME ClearPort: 0.00001 per CHF increment = $1.25
Product Code	CME Globex: 6SCME ClearPort: E1Clearing: E1
Listed Contracts	Quarterly contracts (Mar, Jun, Sep, Dec) listed for 20 consecutive quarters
Settlement Method	Deliverable
Termination of Trading	Trading terminates at 9:16 a.m. CT, 2 business day prior to the third Wednesday of the contract month.

Table 4.1: CME Swiss franc futures specifications [15]

trading, while CME ClearPort is preferred for non-standard, privately negotiated, or OTC contracts that need clearing.

The CME Swiss franc is a quarterly contract expiring in March, June, September and December. Twenty consecutive quarters are listed which means that in October 2024 there are contracts expiring every quarter from December 2024 to September 2029.

The contract specification also states that the contract is deliverable (see chapter 7) and that the last trading day is 2 business days prior to the third Wednesday of the contract month. So, for instance, for December 2024, the third Wednesday is the 18th and so the last trading day is Monday the 16th of December 2024.

Another example, shown in Table 4.2, is the DAX futures contract [16], which represents the German stock market index DAX [30], and is traded on Eurex (see Section 8.1 fr a list of exchanges).

At the moment of writing this paragraph DAX futures value was 19,375. This means that the price of going long or short 1 lot of this contract is $25 \times 19,375 = 484,375$ EUR.

In October 2024 there were 12 quarterly contracts listed from December 2024 to September 2027.

For the contract ending December 2024 the last trading day is the 20th of December 2024.

Contract Value:	25 EUR per point.
Contract Months:	Standard - up to 9 months: The three nearest quarterly months of the March, June, September and December cycle.
Minimum Price Fluctuation:	1 point, 25 EUR.
Last Trading Day:	Last trading day is the final settlement day. Final settlement day is the third Friday of each maturity month if this is an exchange day; otherwise the exchange day immediately preceding that day.
Settlement:	Cash settlement, payable on the first exchange day following the final settlement day.
Trading Hours:	01:10 to 22:00 CET.

Table 4.2: Eurex DAX futures contract specifications [16]

Chapter 5

Market participants

Futures contracts are primarily used by two types of market participants: hedgers, who seek protection from price fluctuations, and speculators, who aim to profit from those fluctuations.

To give an example, one of the products that can be sold and bought as a futures contract is cotton [4] listed on the CME (see section 8.1 for a list of exchanges). Imagine we are at the beginning of August and that the cotton farmer's harvest will be ready, in about 90 days, at the end of October (see figure 5.1 for cotton's futures contract specifications).

If the cotton price falls by the end of October, the farmer will earn less than if they had locked in today's price by selling futures contracts. Conversely, if the cotton price rises, the farmer would miss out on a higher income by having pre-sold at today's rate.

Contract Unit	50,000 pounds
Price Quotation	U.S. Dollars per pound
Trading Hours	CME Globex: Sunday - Friday 6:00 p.m. - 5:00 p.m. (5:00 p.m. - 4:00 p.m. Chicago Time/CT) with a 60-minute break each day beginning at 5:00 p.m. (4:00 p.m. CT) CME ClearPort: Sunday - Friday 6:00 p.m. - 5:00 p.m. (5:00 p.m. - 4:00 p.m. Chicago Time/CT) with a 60-minute break each day beginning at 5:00 p.m. (4:00 p.m. CT)
Minimum Price Fluctuation	$0.0001 per pound
Product Code	CME Globex: TTCME ClearPort: TTClearing: TT
Listed Contracts	Trading is conducted in the March, May, July, October, and December cycle for the next 24 months.
Settlement Method	Financially Settled
Termination of Trading	Trading terminates on the day immediately preceding the first notice day of the corresponding trading month of Cotton futures at ICE Futures U.S.

Table 5.1: CME cotton futures specifications [4]

For the purchaser of cotton, let's say a jeans manufacturing company, the effect is exactly the reverse.

Why do farmers and manufactures enter futures contracts if it is possible to make less money than otherwise? Because they eliminate the risk of price fluctuation. In this example the seller and buyer can plan for the future knowing exactly how much money they are going to pay/receive.

Speculators are individuals or entities that enter into futures contracts with the goal of profiting from price movements in the market, rather than using the contracts to hedge or manage the risk of an existing position in a physical asset. Unlike hedgers, speculators have no underlying exposure to the commodity or financial asset they are trading—they are purely focused on the potential for gain (or loss) from price movements.

In summary:

- Hedgers use futures to manage or mitigate risk in their underlying business or investments. They aim to protect themselves from price fluctuations in commodities, currencies, or financial assets that they are exposed to. Hedgers take a position in the futures market that is opposite to their exposure in the physical or cash market. For example, an oats farmer might sell oats futures contracts [12] listed on CME (see section 8.1 for a list of exchanges) to lock in a price for their upcoming crop, protecting against the risk of falling prices at harvest. Typical example of hedgers are:
    - Farmers

- manufacturers
- importers/exporters
- any corporations with exposure to commodities, interest rates, or foreign exchange rates.

- Speculators trade futures to profit from price movements, not to manage existing exposure to an asset. They aim to buy low and sell high (or sell high and buy low) to capture gains from changes in market prices. Speculators assume risk by taking either long (buy) or short (sell) positions in the futures market, depending on their predictions about future price movements. Unlike hedgers, they don't produce or consume the underlying asset; they are only interested in capitalizing on market volatility. Example of speculators are:

  - individual traders,
  - investment funds,
  - proprietary trading firms that actively buy and sell futures contracts.

In conclusion:

- Hedgers seek protection from price changes, while speculators seek to profit from those changes.

- Hedgers aim to reduce risk, whereas speculators willingly take on risk for potential profit.

- Hedgers are typically connected to the physical commodity or financial asset, while speculators often have no connection to the underlying asset other than the trade.

	Producer/User		Swap Dealers			Managed Money			Other Reportables		
	Long	Short	Long	Short	Spreading	Long	Short	Spreading	Long	Short	Spreading
Positions	365,386	556,180	261,964	13,992	33,880	209,082	281,167	250,070	112,219	47,327	117,990
% of OI	24.6	37.5	17.7	0.9	2.3	14.1	18.9	16.8	7.6	3.2	7.9
# traders	266	286	26	8	17	67	76	87	79	64	77

Table 5.2: Excerpt from the Commitment of Traders report [1] for Corn futures on October 1, 2024, showing position distribution across different trader categories.

Both hedgers and speculators are essential to the futures markets: hedgers provide stability, while speculators provide liquidity by actively trading, which makes it easier for hedgers to enter or exit positions. This balance keeps futures markets functioning effectively.

The balance between hedgers and speculators varies across markets. A key resource is the Commitment of Traders Report [1] released weekly by the Commodity Futures Trading Commission (CFTC). Although released on Fridays, the report generally reflects positions as of the preceding Tuesday.

Table 5.2 is an extract from the Commitment of Traders report for the corn futures contract [3] listed on the CME (see section 8.1 for a list of exchanges) reported for the 1st October, 2024. This table shows positions, percent of open interest and number of trades per type of user. The total open interest (OI) reported was 1,484,174 (note that not all positions are reported).

Open interest is the total number of outstanding futures contracts that have not been settled. Open interest keeps track of every open position in a contract rather than tracking the total volume traded.

As it can be seen in Table 5.2, 24.6% of long positions (buyers) and

37.5% of short positions (sellers) are hedgers (producers or users). The remaining open interest is held by speculators.

Chapter 6

Margins and daily settlement

At the start of a futures transaction, no money changes hands in terms of the full contract value. Neither the buyer pays for the contracts they purchase, nor does the seller receive payment for the contracts they sell.

Instead, exchanges require traders to post a portion of a contract's value, known as margin. The specific margin amount is influenced by both exchange requirements and broker criteria, with brokers often adjusting based on their risk assessment of individual clients.

Margins are then "Marked to Market", meaning they are adjusted daily (and sometimes intraday) based on current market prices. When the market price moves, funds flow between the buyer's and seller's margin accounts to reflect the gain or loss.

For example, assume we hold a long position on a British Pound (GBP) futures contract [2], listed on the CME (see section 8.1 for a list of exchanges), bought yesterday at the price of 1.31 USD for 1 GBP. In this circumstances the value of 1 lot is $1.31 \times 62,500 = 81,875$ USD (see table 6.1 for the CME GBP contract specification). Lets imagine that today the price is 1.30. Now the value of this contract is $1.30 \times 62,500 = 81,250$ USD. This represents a loss for the long position of 625 USD. Therefore the buyer's margin account will be deducted by this amount, while the seller's account (the short position) will be increased.

This flow from one margin account to the other is done via a clearinghouse (see section 8.2 for a list of the main clearinghouses) as buyer and seller do not know each other.

There are two main types of margins:

- Initial Margin: This is the minimum amount of capital required to open a futures position. This is meant to ensure the trader can cover potential losses. For instance, if a trader buys a coffee futures contract [24] on ICE (see Section 8.1 for a list of exchnages) with a 20% initial margin requirement, they would need to deposit 20% of the contract's total value to open a position.

- Maintenance Margin: This is the minimum balance the trader must maintain in his/hers account once the trade is open. If the account balance drops below the maintenance margin due to daily losses, the trader would receive a margin call to bring

Contract Unit	62,500 British pounds
Price Quotation	U.S. dollars and cents per GBP increment
Trading Hours	CME Globex: Sunday - Friday 6:00 p.m. - 5:00 p.m. (5:00 p.m. - 4:00 p.m. CT) with a 60-minute break each day beginning at 5:00 p.m. (4:00 p.m. CT) CME ClearPort: Sunday 5:00 p.m. - Friday 5:45 p.m. CT with no reporting Monday - Thursday from 5:45 p.m. - 6:00 p.m. CT
Minimum Price Fluctuation	CME Globex: 0.0001 per GBP increments = $6.25 Spreads: 0.00005 per GBP increment = $3.125 CME ClearPort: 0.00001 per GBP increment = $0.625
Product Code	CME Globex: 6BCME ClearPort: BPClearing: BP
Listed Contracts	Quarterly contracts (Mar, Jun, Sep, Dec) listed for 20 consecutive quarters and serial contracts listed for 3 months
Settlement Method	Deliverable
Termination of Trading	Trading terminates at 9:16 a.m. CT, 2 business days prior to the third Wednesday of the contract month.

Table 6.1: CME British Pound Futures Specifications [2]

the balance back up to the initial margin level. This ensures that there is always enough capital to cover potential losses. If a trader can't answer a margin call the trader's positions will be closed and the account terminated.

In summary the Daily Settlement or Mark to Market process is where futures contracts are settled at the end of each trading day based on their closing prices. The purpose is to track gains or losses in real-time and ensure that accounts are adjusted daily. The Mark to Market process works as follows:

- Marking to Market: at the end of each trading day, the exchange calculates the difference between the contract's opening price and its closing price. Any gain or loss from the day's price movement is added or deducted from the trader's margin account.

- Daily gain or loss: if the contract's value increased, the long position (the buyer) gains and the short position (the seller) loses. If the value decreased, the long position loses and the short position gains.

- Margin calls: if losses reduce your balance below the maintenance margin, the trader will receive a *margin call*. The trader must deposit more funds to bring the balance back to the initial margin level. Failure to meet a margin call may force the exchange to close the trader's position to cover potential losses, preventing further exposure.

In conclusion, margins and daily settlement protect both the trader and the exchange by ensuring that participants can cover their obligations. Daily settlements keep the market stable and liquid by ensuring all traders are continually in good financial standing, avoiding large unpaid losses. Daily Mark to Market accounting gives all participants up-to-date information on their positions and the market's direction.

6.1 Leverage and Risks in Futures Trading

One of the distinguishing features of futures contracts is the use of leverage. Leverage allows traders to control a large position in an asset with a relatively small upfront investment, the margin. This means that a trader can gain exposure to the full value of the asset without paying the total price upfront. While leverage can magnify gains, it also amplifies losses, making risk management essential.

Let's consider for example, a trader that enters a futures contract of Crude oil [5] trade on CME (see table 6.2 for the CME crude oil futures contract specifications).

The trader goes long 1 lot of crude oil at 70 USD per barrel. The value of this lot is $70 \times 1,000 = 70,000$ USD. The trader will only pay a fraction of this value, let's say 15%, which is 10,500 USD.

If the price rises to 75 USD, the trader profits from the entire 5 USD increase per barrel, even though they only invested a fraction of the contract's value as margin. This means the trader made 5,000 USD from a 10,500 USD investment. A very interesting return.

Contract Unit	1,000 barrels
Price Quotation	U.S. dollars and cents per barrel
Trading Hours	CME Globex: Sunday - Friday 5:00 p.m. - 4:00 p.m. CT with a 60-minute break each day beginning at 4:00 p.m. CT TAS: Sunday - Friday 5:00 p.m. - 1:30 p.m. CT CME ClearPort: Sunday 5:00 p.m. - Friday 4:00 p.m. CT with no reporting Monday - Thursday from 4:00 p.m. - 5:00 p.m. CT
Minimum Price Fluctuation	0.01 per barrel = $10.00 TAS: Zero or +/- 10 ticks in the minimum tick increment of the outright
Product Code	CME Globex:CL CME ClearPort:CLC learing: CL TAS: CLT TAM: "CLS","CLC","CLL"
Listed Contracts	Monthly contracts listed for the current year and the next 10 calendar years and 2 additional contract months. List monthly contracts for a new calendar year and 2 additional contract months following the termination of trading in the December contract of the current year.
Settlement Method	Deliverable
Termination of Trading	Trading terminates 3 business day before the 25th calendar day of the month prior to the contract month. If the 25th calendar day is not a business day, trading terminates 4 business days before the 25th calendar day of the month prior to the contract month.

Table 6.2: CME Crude oil Futures Specifications [5]

However, if the price drops to 65 USD, the trader incurs a 5 USD per barrel loss, 5,000 USD in total, losing almost half of the initial margin. In this circumstance, almost certainly the trader would be required to deposit more funds or risk liquidation.

In conclusion even a small price change can have a significant impact on the trader's account. Traders are advised to carefully manage leverage by monitoring market conditions and maintaining an appropriate amount of capital in their accounts to cover potential losses.

Chapter 7

Settlement and delivery

In the futures market, delivery refers to the actual transfer of the underlying asset (commodity or financial instrument) from the seller to the buyer when the futures contract reaches its expiration.

There are two types of delivery mechanisms in the futures market: physical delivery and cash settlement.

For example a wheat producer sells a contract of milling wheat #2 futures [17] listed on Euronext (see section 8.1 for a list of exchanges). Table 7.1 shows this contract specifications.

The producer's objective is to protect himself/herself against price fluctuations (see chapter 5). At the expiration date the producer will have to deliver the wheat.

Contract Code	EBM
Unit of trading	Fifty tonnes
Price Quotation	Euro and euro cents per tonne
Origins Tenderable	European Union
Quality	Sound, fair and merchantable quality of: - the following minimum specifications: · Hagberg falling number: 220 seconds · Protein content: 11% dry matter · Specific weight: 76 kg/hl and - the following basis specifications: · Moisture content: 15% · Broken grains: 4% · Impurities: 2% Discounts apply to reflect any difference between the delivered and standard quality, in accordance with Incograin No.23 and the Technical Addendum No.2. Please also refer to the rules and regulation below for more details. Mycotoxins not to exceed, at the time of delivery, the maximum levels specified under EU legislation in force with respect to unprocessed cereals intended for use in food products.
Minimum Price Movement	25 euro cents per tonne (€12.50)
Delivery Months	September, December, March, May such that 12 delivery months are available for trading.
Last trading day	18:30 on the tenth calendar day of the delivery month (if not a business day, then the following business day)
Settlement (Delivery)	In an approved silo in Dunkirk, La Pallice, Montoir, Nantes or Rouen (France)
Trading hours	10:45 – 18:30 CET

Table 7.1: Euronext Milling Wheat Futures Specifications [17]

As we can see in table 7.1, the delivery can occur on any business day from the last trading day through the end of the specified delivery month. For example, if the producer sold the September 2024 contract, they would have from the last trading day, September 10, to the end of the month, September 30, to make the delivery.

The delivery will be to an approved silo in Dunkirk, La Pallice, Montoir, Nantes or Rouen. This is an example of physical delivery.

Let's consider another example. One investor wants to buy the S&P 500 index in 3 months. The investor has the cash now and wants to hedge himself/herself, that is to protect himself/herself against price variations. The investor can buy E-mini S&P 500 contracts [8] traded on CME (see section 8.1 for a list of exchanges). The E-mini S&P 500 contract specification are shown in table 7.2.

At the expiry date, 3rd Friday of the contract month, the investor will not receive stocks of the S&P 500 index components. The investor margin account (see chapter 6) will have increased/decreased by the investor's profit/loss.

Let's imagine that the investor buys today 1 contract (also called 1 lot) of the March 2025 contract which is worth 5798.00 points. The value of this contract is 50 USD $\times$ 5798 = 289, 900 USD. Let's imagine that at the expiration date the S&P Index is worth 5852.00 points. The value of this contract is now 50 USD $\times$ 5852 = 292, 600 USD. The investor instead of receiving the S&P 500 index components will have profited 292, 600 − 289, 400 = 2700 USD. The investor can now go buy the S&P index components if he/she so wishes (not an easy task). This an example of cash settlement.

Contract Unit	$50 × S&P 500 Index
Price Quotation	U.S. dollars and cents per index point
Trading Hours	CME Globex: Sunday 6:00 p.m. - Friday - 5:00 p.m. ET (5:00 p.m. - 4:00 p.m. CT) with a daily maintenance period from 5:00 p.m. - 6:00 p.m. ET (4:00 p.m. - 5:00 p.m. CT) TACO: Sunday - Friday 6:00 p.m. - 9:30 a.m. ET. Monday - Friday 11:00 a.m. - 5:00 p.m. ET with a daily maintenance period 5:00 p.m. - 6:00 p.m. ET BTIC: Sunday - Friday 6:00 p.m. - 4:00 p.m. ET TMAC: Sunday - Friday 6:00 p.m. - 4:00 p.m. ET CME ClearPort: Sunday 6:00 p.m. - Friday 6:45 p.m. ET (Sun 5:00 - Fri 5:45 p.m. CT) with no reporting Monday - Thursday 6:45 p.m. - 7:00 p.m. ET (5:45 p.m. - 6:00 p.m. CT) TACO: Sunday 6:00 p.m. - Monday 9:30 a.m. ET. Monday - Thursday 11:00 a.m. - 5:00 p.m. ET and 6:00 p.m. - 9:30 a.m. ET BTIC: Sunday - Friday 6:00 p.m. - 4:00 p.m. ET. BTICs for the following trading day can be submitted after 7:00 p.m. ET (6:00 p.m. CT) TMAC: Sunday - Friday 6:00 p.m. - 4:00 p.m. ET. TMACs for the following trading day can be submitted after 7:00 p.m. ET (6:00 p.m. CT)
Minimum Price Fluctuation	0.25 index points = $12.50 TACO: 0.05 index points = $2.50 BTIC: 0.05 index points = $2.50 TMAC: 0.05 index points = $2.50 Zero or +/- 20 ticks (4 futures ticks) around the Market at Close price of the outright CALENDAR SPREAD: 0.05 index points = $2.50
Product Code	CME Globex: ES CME ClearPort: ES Clearing: ES BTIC: EST TACO: ESQ TMAC: ESX
Listed Contracts	Quarterly contracts (Mar, Jun, Sep, Dec) listed for 21 consecutive quarters BTIC & TACO: Eligible in all listed contract months TMAC: Eligible in the contract month nearest to expiry. The next quarterly TMAC is eligible for trading on Sunday of the week of the prior contract month's expiration.
Settlement Method	Financially Settled
Termination of Trading	Trading terminates at 9:30 a.m. ET on the 3rd Friday of the contract month. TACO trading terminates at 9:30 a.m. ET on the Thursday before the 3rd Friday of the contract month. BTIC trading terminates at 4:00 p.m. ET on the Thursday before the 3rd Friday of contract month. TMAC trading terminates at 4:00 p.m. ET on the Thursday before the 3rd Friday of the contract month.

Table 7.2: CME E-mini S&P 500 futures Specifications [8]

Typically futures contracts are either physically delivered or cash settled. In some rare occasions, like the Brent Crude Futures traded on ICE (see chapter 8.1 for a list of exchanges), both are acceptable.

Dual settlement options are designed to make futures contracts more versatile and accessible to a broader audience. By offering both options, exchanges can attract both commercial entities needing the physical asset and speculative or financial participants who prefer the simplicity of cash settlement.

In summary:

- Physical Delivery involves the actual delivery of the commodity or asset upon expiration. Physical delivery contracts are common for commodities like agricultural products, metals, and energy.

- Cash Settlement, meaning no physical asset changes hands. Instead, the contract is settled by a payment based on the final price of the asset at expiration. Cash settlement contracts are common for financial instruments like stock indices or interest rates.

Important dates on the delivery process are:

- First Notice Day is the first day on which a seller can notify their intention to deliver the asset or the buyer can notify (not always required and may not even be necessary in most cases) the desire to take deliver.

- Last Trading Day is the last day a futures contract can be traded before entering the delivery process. Positions still open after this day will go to delivery.

- Delivery Date is the actual date on which the delivery occurs, as specified in the contract. For physically settled contracts, this is when the seller provides the asset and the buyer receives it.

Market participates (see chapter 5 for a more detailed discussion) and delivery:

- Commercial and institutional participants (hedgers): farmers, manufacturers, or companies that use the commodity often engage in physical delivery.

- Speculators and traders: most speculators exit before the delivery date to avoid the logistical hassle of receiving or delivering the actual asset.

Delivery ensures futures markets remain connected to the actual supply and demand for the underlying asset. By having the option of physical delivery, futures prices closely track the real market value, which benefits both hedgers and speculators.

Speculators, and even some hedgers, usually close their positions before the delivery date to avoid the logistics of receiving or delivering the actual asset. Closing a position means that if they hold a long position, they would sell it, and if they hold a short position, they would buy it back.

In fact it is estimated that, for most futures markets, fewer than 2-3% of contracts result in actual delivery of the underlying asset. The reason is that from the logistics point of view is not necessarily easy for the producer to deliver the product or for the manufacturer to take delivery.

So how does it work? For instance, imagine a producer of white sugar who knows, in October 2024, that they will have 100 tons to sell in December 2024. The producer is worried of a price drop and decides to sell two white sugar futures contracts [25] traded on ICE, for 563 USD per ton, to hedge against price fluctuations (see Chapter 5). Table 7.3 shows ICE white sugar futures contracts specifications.

As the delivery date approaches, let's consider two possible scenarios:

- White sugar's market price has fallen to 560. The futures market profit is $2 \times 50 \times (563 - 560) = 300$ USD The producer now sells the the sugar on the market for 560 USD per ton making $560 \times 100 = 56000$ USD. So the total income for the producer will be $56000 + 300 = 56300$ USD or 563 USD per ton.

- White sugar's market price has risen to 567. The futures market loss is $2 \times 50 \times (567 - 563) = 400$ USD The producer now sells the the sugar on the market for 567 USD per ton making $567 \times 100 = 56700$ USD. So the total income for the producer will be $56700 - 400 = 56300$ USD or 563 USD per ton.

So, in the example above, the producer was able to fix the white sugar's price at 563 USD per ton without having to physically deliver

Contract Symbol	W
Contract Size	Fifty Tonnes
Price Quotation	Dollars and cents per metric tonne
Contract Series	March, May, August, October, December, such that fourteen delivery months are available for trading
Minimum Price Fluctuation	10 cents per tonne ($5)
Settlement	Physical Delivery
Delivery Locations	FOB and stowed in vessel's hold in a port residing in one of the Deliverable Countries of Production listed below and which meets the requirements of the Exchange: Algeria, Argentina, Australia, Austria, Belgium, Brazil, Bulgaria, Canada, Chile, China, Colombia, Croatia, Czechia, Denmark, Egypt, El Salvador, Finland, France, Germany, Guatemala, Hungary, India, Italy, Korea (Republic of), Lithuania, Malaysia, Mauritius, Mexico, Morocco, Mozambique, The Netherlands, Pakistan, Peru, Poland, Philippines, Portugal, Romania, Saudi Arabia, Slovakia, South Africa, Spain, Sudan, Sweden, Thailand, Turkey, U.A.E., United Kingdom, U.S.A., Vietnam
Grade/Standards/Quality	White beet, cane crystal sugar or refined sugar of the crop or production current on the first day of the delivery period, free running of regular grain size and fair average of the quality of deliveries made from the declared origin from such crop or production, with minimum polarisation 99.8 degrees, moisture maximum 0.06%, and colour of a maximum of 45 units ICUMSA attenuation index at time of delivery to vessel at the port.
Deliverable Origins	White beet or cane crystal sugar or refined sugar of the crop or production current on the first day of the delivery period
First Notice Day	Fifteen calendar days preceding the first day of the delivery period (if not a business day then the first business day following). Delivery period is the specified delivery month and the following delivery month.
Last Trading Day	Sixteen calendar days preceding the first day of the delivery month at 17:55 (if not a business day then the first business day immediately preceding)
Last Notice Day	Fifteen calendar days preceding the first day of the delivery period (if not a business day then the first business day following). Delivery period is the specified delivery month and the following delivery month.
Trading Hours	New York: 03:45 - 13:00 London: 08:45 - 18:00 Singapore: 16:45 - 02:00

Table 7.3: ICE white sugar futures contracts specifications [25]

Month	Code
January	F
Frebruary	G
March	H
April	J
May	K
June	M
July	N
August	Q
September	U
October	V
November	X
December	Z

Table 7.4: Futures month codes

the product. Note that close to delivery time the market price (spot price) and the futures price tend to be the same.

Futures contracts are assigned a code to represent each delivery month, as shown in Table 7.4. These codes are standardized across futures markets to simplify contract identification.

Chapter 8

Futures exchanges and clearinghouses

8.1 Futures exchanges

A futures exchange is a regulated and transparent market where futures contracts and other derivatives are traded, that is they can be bought and sold.

The general public does not have direct access to exchanges and only brokers and other members of the exchange are allowed to trade. This means that the public can only trade futures though a broker. Note that when I say public I am not just referring to individuals. Hedge funds, pension funds, insurance companies and other institutional investors also must use brokers, unless they are exchange members.

Some of the largest futures exchanges are:

- Chicago Mercantil Exchange (CME group) in the United States. The largest futures exchange in the world, CME Group includes the Chicago Mercantile Exchange, Chicago Board of Trade (CBOT), New York Mercantile Exchange (NYMEX) and The Commodity Exchange (COMEX). It offers a wide range of contracts, including agricultural products, energy, metals, interest rates, and equity indexes.

- Intercontinental Exchange (ICE) in both United States and Europe. ICE is a major global exchange that operates futures markets in North America, Europe, and Asia. ICE Futures U.S. is prominent for its soft commodities like coffee, sugar, and cotton, while ICE Futures Europe is known for Brent crude oil futures.

- Eurex in Germany. Based in Frankfurt, Eurex is one of Europe's largest futures exchanges, specializing in European equity index and fixed-income derivatives. It's particularly known for the Euro Stoxx 50 Index futures and Bund (German government bond) futures.

- Shanghai Futures Exchange (SHFE) in China. SHFE is one of the largest futures exchanges in Asia, focusing on metals, energy, and other commodities. It's notable for its copper, aluminium, and steel rebar futures, which play a crucial role in global metals trading.

- Japan Exchange Group also known as TOCOM in Japan, specializes in energy and metals, particularly gold and crude oil futures, and is a major player in the Asian commodities market.

- Multi Commodity Exchange (MCX) in India. MCX is known for trading metals and energy, including gold, silver, crude oil, and natural gas futures, and is one of the largest commodity exchanges in the region.

- Brazilian Mercantile and Futures Exchange (BM&F Bovespa) in Brazil. Now part of B3 (Brasil, Bolsa, Balcao), it's the largest futures exchange in Latin America, with products in agricultural and financial futures, such as the Ibovespa Index and coffee futures.

- Euronext in Europe. Euronext is one of the largest exchanges in Europe, with a strong presence in both the stock and futures markets. While it's primarily known as a major stock exchange operating across European cities like Paris, Amsterdam, Brussels, Dublin, Lisbon, and Oslo, Euronext also operates a robust derivatives market, particularly focused on equity and index futures.

- The Singapore Exchange (SGX) is one of Asia's leading derivatives and securities exchange, based in Singapore. SGX plays a significant role in global futures trading, especially for products tied to Asian markets and commodities. It's widely respected for its robust international market access and the liquidity it provides, particularly for investors looking to trade Asia-Pacific assets.

- Hong Kong Exchanges and Clearing (HKEX) in Hong Kong, China. HKEX is a major exchange for both securities and derivatives, acting as a bridge between Chinese and international markets. HKEX is particularly valuable to global investors seeking exposure to Mainland China.

- Korea Exchange (KRX) in South Korea. KRX is a comprehensive exchange with significant activity in derivatives, offering exposure to South Korea's economy and global trading interests. It's a vital platform for trading both equity-linked and commodity derivatives.

8.2 Clearinghouses

Clearinghouses are crucial for the smooth operation of futures markets. They act as intermediaries between buyers and sellers, ensuring the integrity and stability of all transactions.

Clearinghouse's main roles are:

- Counterparty risk mitigation: the clearinghouse is the counterparty to both sides of every trade, guaranteeing the transaction. This process, known as novation, means that the clearinghouse steps in so that the buyer doesn't have to worry about the seller's solvency and vice versa.

- Manage daily settlements: clearinghouses manage the daily Mark to Market process (see chapter 6), ensuring that profits and losses are settled daily. They calculate gains or losses on all open positions and adjust the accounts of all traders accordingly.

- Manage margin requirements: manage both initial and maintenance margins and enforce margin calls when necessary (see chapter 6). This reduces the risk of unpaid losses and keeps participants accountable for their positions.

- Ensuring financial stability in the markets: they maintain guarantee funds (pools of funds from clearing members) to cover potential defaults and require members to meet strict financial and operational standards.

- Ensuring operational efficiency and transparency: clearinghouses standardize and streamline transaction processes, enhancing efficiency and transparency. This includes the settlement of contracts, delivery when physical settlement is required (see chapter 7), and record-keeping.

Some of the largest clearing houses are:

- CME Clearing: part of CME Group, which includes the Chicago Mercantile Exchange, CME Clearing is one of the world's largest clearinghouses. It clears a vast range of products, including agricultural, metals, interest rate, and currency futures.

- ICE Clear: ICE operates multiple clearinghouses globally, including ICE Clear U.S., ICE Clear Europe, and ICE Clear Singapore. ICE Clear handles products in energy, financials, and soft commodities and is a key player in derivatives clearing.

- LCH.Clearnet part of the LCH Group (United Kingdom and Europe): is owned by the London Stock Exchange Group, is one of Europe's leading clearinghouses. It clears interest rate swaps, forex contracts, and other derivatives and is especially known for its SwapClear service for interest rate swaps.

- Japan Securities Clearing Corporation (JSCC) in Japan: is the main clearinghouse for Japan, clearing financial derivatives, equities, and commodities for the Tokyo Stock Exchange and Osaka Exchange.

- Eurex Clearing part of Deutsche Börse Group (Germany): Eurex Clearing provides clearing services for Eurex derivatives, including equity and index futures, fixed-income products, and commodities. It is one of the largest clearinghouses in Europe and plays a crucial role in European financial markets.

- Shanghai Futures Exchange Clearing House (SHFE) part of the Shanghai Futures Exchange (China): this clearinghouse operates in China, supporting futures contracts on commodities like metals, energy, and agricultural products, primarily catering to the Asian market.

In conclusion, clearinghouses add a layer of security and confidence to futures markets, allowing traders to engage without worrying about default risks.

Chapter 9

Final remarks

Hopefully after reading this book you, the reader, will have a good understanding of basic futures concepts, namely:

- The definition of a future contract.

- Main differences between futures and forward (maturity and standardization).

- The types of products that can be traded: commodities and financials.

- Futures markets specification, which standardize every aspect of the contract.

- Who are the market participants and for what purposes hedging and speculating can be used.

- Understand the importance of margins and daily settlement as a way of guaranteeing traders are solvent.

- The importance of risk management as futures are leveraged products.

- The difference between physical delivery and cash settlement.

- Have an idea which are the main exchanges and clearinghouses and their role in the market.

Bibliography

[1] Commodity Futures Trading Commission (CFTC). *Commitments of Traders*. Accessed 2024-11-12. URL: https://www.cftc.gov/MarketReports/CommitmentsofTraders/index.htm.

[2] CME. *British Pound*. Accessed 2024-11-12. URL: https://www.cmegroup.com/markets/fx/g10/british-pound.contractSpecs.html.

[3] CME. *Corn*. Accessed 2024-11-10. URL: https://www.cmegroup.com/markets/agriculture/grains/corn.contractSpecs.html.

[4] CME. *Cotton*. Accessed 2024-11-09. URL: https://www.cmegroup.com/markets/agriculture/lumber-and-softs/cotton.contractSpecs.html.

[5] CME. *Crude Oil*. Accessed 2024-11-11. URL: https://www.cmegroup.com/markets/energy/crude-oil/light-sweet-crude.contractSpecs.html.

[6] CME. *DAX® Futures (FDAX)*. Accessed 2024-11-08. URL: https://www.cmegroup.com/markets/energy/natural-gas/natural-gas.contractSpecs.html.

[7] CME. *E-mini Nasdaq-100*. Accessed 2024-11-08. URL: https://www.cmegroup.com/markets/equities/nasdaq/e-mini-nasdaq-100.contractSpecs.html.

[8] CME. *E-mini S&P 500*. Accessed 2024-11-15. URL: https://www.cmegroup.com/markets/equities/sp/e-mini-sandp500.contractSpecs.html.

[9] CME. *Euro FX*. Accessed 2024-11-08. URL: https://www.cmegroup.com/markets/fx/g10/euro-fx.contractSpecs.html.

[10] CME. *Gold*. Accessed 2024-11-08. URL: https://www.cmegroup.com/markets/metals/precious/gold.contractSpecs.html.

[11] CME. *Mexican Peso*. Accessed 2024-11-08. URL: https://www.cmegroup.com/markets/fx/emerging-market/mexican-peso.contractSpecs.html.

[12] CME. *Oats*. Accessed 2024-11-09. URL: https://www.cmegroup.com/markets/agriculture/grains/oats.contractSpecs.html.

[13] CME. *Platinum*. Accessed 2024-11-08. URL: https://www.cmegroup.com/markets/metals/precious/platinum.contractSpecs.html.

[14] CME. *Rough Rice*. Accessed 2024-11-14. URL: https://www.cmegroup.com/markets/agriculture/grains/rough-rice.contractSpecs.html.

[15] CME. *Swiss Franc*. Accessed 2024-11-14. URL: https://www.cmegroup.com/markets/fx/g10/swiss-franc.contractSpecs.html.

[16] Eurex. *DAX*. Accessed 2024-11-09. URL: https://www.eurex.com/ex-en/markets/idx/dax/DAX-Futures-139902.

[17] EURONEXT. *Milling Wheat / Ble de Meunerie*. Accessed 2024-11-08. URL: https://live.euronext.com/en/product/commodities-futures/EBM-DPAR/contract-specification.

[18] EURONEXT. *Rapeseed / Colza*. Accessed 2024-11-08. URL: https://live.euronext.com/en/product/commodities-futures/ECO-DPAR/contract-specification.

[19] HKEX. *Hang Seng Index Futures*. Accessed 2024-11-08. URL: https://www.hkex.com.hk/Products/Listed-Derivatives/Equity-Index/Hang-Seng-Index-(HSI)/Hang-Seng-Index-Futures?sc_lang=en#&product=HSI.

[20] ICE. *CE Futures U.S. Cocoa Futures*. Accessed 2024-11-08. URL: https://www.ice.com/products/7/Cocoa-Futures.

[21] ICE. *FCOJ-A Futures*. Accessed 2024-11-10. URL: https://www.ice.com/products/30/FCOJ-A-Futures.

[22] ICE. *Long Gilt Future*. Accessed 2024-11-08. URL: https://www.ice.com/products/37650336/Long-Gilt-Future.

[23] ICE. *Low Sulphur Gasoil Futures*. Accessed 2024-11-08. URL: https://www.ice.com/products/34361119/low-sulphur-gasoil-futures.

[24] ICE. *Robusta Coffee Futures*. Accessed 2024-11-12. URL: https://www.ice.com/products/37089079/Robusta-Coffee-Futures.

[25] ICE. *White Sugar Futures*. Accessed 2024-11-15. URL: https://www.ice.com/products/37089080/White-Sugar-Futures.

[26] JPX. *RSS3 Rubber Futures*. Accessed 2024-11-10. URL: https://www.jpx.co.jp/english/derivatives/products/rubber/rss3-rubber-futures/01.html.

[27] KRX. *KOSPI 200 Futures*. Accessed 2024-11-10. URL: https://global.krx.co.kr/contents/GLB/02/0201/0201040201/GLB0201040201.jsp.

[28] MCX. *MCX Metal & Energy*. Accessed 2024-11-09. URL: https://www.mcxindia.com.

[29] SGX. *SGX 10 Year Full-sized Japanese Government Bond Futures*. Accessed 2024-11-08. URL: https://www.sgx.com/derivatives/products/jgb?cc=JG#Contract%20Specifications.

[30] STOXX. *DAX*. Accessed 2024-11-09. URL: https://stoxx.com/index/dax/.

www.ingramcontent.com/pod-product-compliance
Lightning Source LLC
Chambersburg PA
CBHW050310220526
45465CB00005B/1935